THE CIVIL WAR
THE FINAL YEARS

BY JIM OLLHOFF

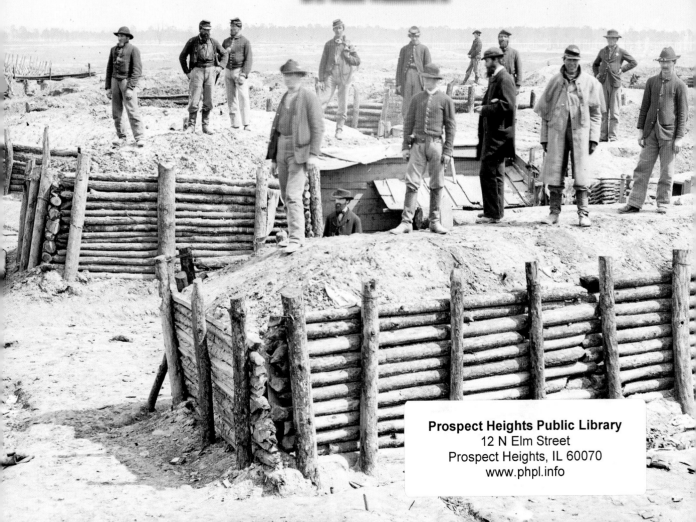

VISIT US AT
WWW.ABDOPUBLISHING.COM

Printed in the United States of America, North Mankato, Minnesota.
122011
012012

 PRINTED ON RECYCLED PAPER

Editor: John Hamilton
Graphic Design: Sue Hamilton
Cover Design: Neil Klinepier
Cover Photo: Getty
Interior Photos and Illustrations: Corbis-pgs 10-11, 24 & 27; Getty-pgs 8-9, 14-15, 22-23, 28 &
29; Granger Collection-pgs 7 & 28 (top inset); Hal Jespersen, www.posix.com/cw-original maps
pgs 9, 11, 17 & 25; John Hamilton-maps on pgs 9, 11, 17 & 25; Library of Congress-pgs 1, 3, 6,
12, 13, 16, 17, 18, 19, 20, 21, & 26; National Archives-pg 12; Thinkstock-pg 5.

ABDO Booklinks
To learn more about the Civil War, visit ABDO Publishing Company online. Web sites about
the Civil War are featured on our Book Links pages. These links are routinely monitored and
updated to provide the most current information available. Web site: www.abdopublishing.com

Library of Congress Cataloging-in-Publication Data

Ollhoff, Jim, 1959-
  The Civil War : the final years / Jim Ollhoff.
     p. cm. -- (The Civil War)
  Includes index.
  ISBN 978-1-61783-274-1
  1. United States--History--Civil War, 1861-1865--Campaigns--Juvenile literature. I. Title. II.
Title: Final years.
  E470.O455 2012
  973.7'34--dc23
                    2011039416

CONTENTS

Soldiers rest after the fall of Atlanta, Georgia.

1864-1865

THE UNION MARCHES TOWARD VICTORY

In 1864 and 1865, both North and South had battlefield victories. However, it became clear that the Union would eventually win the war. There were several reasons for this.

The Union victories at Gettysburg, Pennsylvania, and Vicksburg, Mississippi, were huge blows to the Confederacy. The South never totally recovered from those massive battles. The Union had more soldiers and they were better equipped.

The South compensated with the brilliant military strategy of General Robert. E. Lee, but it wasn't enough.

The Southern economy continued to suffer. Because of the Union's blockade, the South couldn't sell cotton, its main crop. In contrast, the Union's economy continued growing, with advances in manufacturing and the discovery of gold and silver in Nevada.

Confederate and Union soldiers recreate a Civil War battle. As the war progressed, it became clear that the Union would eventually win.

Europe decided not to recognize the South as an independent nation. The Confederacy had hoped that England and France would become Confederate allies, and send their massive armies to help the South. This never happened, and was another huge blow to the Confederacy. England and France did not want to support a nation that allowed slavery.

In September 1862, President Abraham Lincoln announced the Emancipation Proclamation, which declared slaves in rebellious states to be free. The Civil War wasn't just about preserving the Union anymore. It was also a fight against the evils of slavery. This was a powerful motivating force for the North.

The continued passion of the abolitionists, who demanded freedom for all, continued to motivate the North. Leaders such as Frederick Douglass, a former slave, gave a powerful voice for freedom and dignity.

With continued pressure from men like Frederick Douglass, African Americans were eventually allowed to fight for the Union. About 180,000 African Americans became part of the Union army, including both free men and runaway slaves. African American troops proved their battle readiness over and over, even though they had lower pay and a higher casualty rate than white soldiers.

Toward the end of the war, Confederate President Jefferson Davis proposed to arm black slaves and force them to fight, but this proposal was never put into practice.

Many battles would be fought, and many men would die, until the final surrender of the Confederate army in April 1865.

Frederick Douglass

African American Union soldiers celebrate the Emancipation Proclamation.

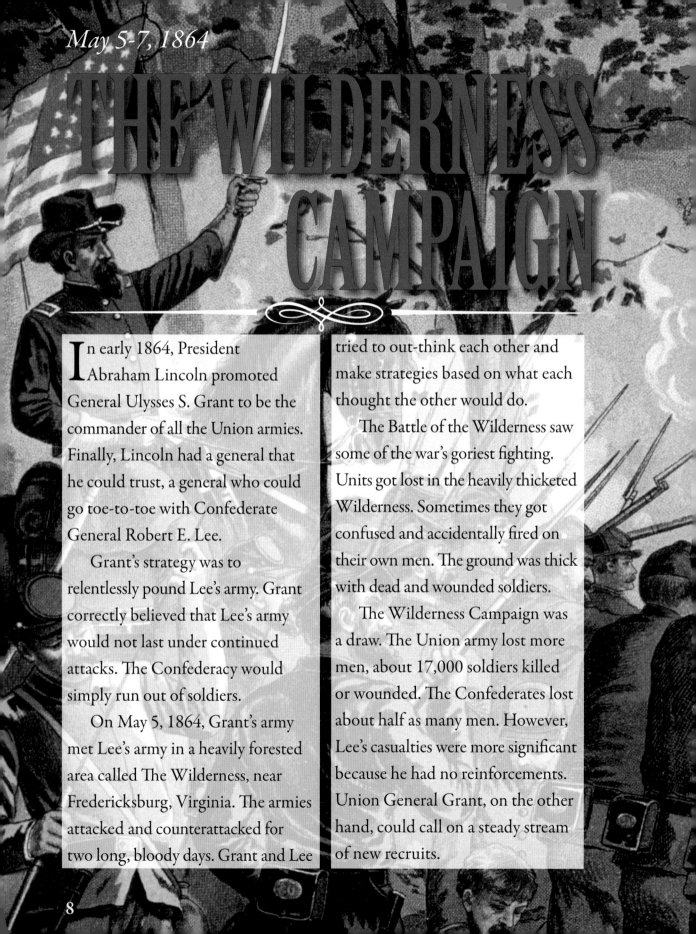

May 5-7, 1864

THE WILDERNESS CAMPAIGN

In early 1864, President Abraham Lincoln promoted General Ulysses S. Grant to be the commander of all the Union armies. Finally, Lincoln had a general that he could trust, a general who could go toe-to-toe with Confederate General Robert E. Lee.

Grant's strategy was to relentlessly pound Lee's army. Grant correctly believed that Lee's army would not last under continued attacks. The Confederacy would simply run out of soldiers.

On May 5, 1864, Grant's army met Lee's army in a heavily forested area called The Wilderness, near Fredericksburg, Virginia. The armies attacked and counterattacked for two long, bloody days. Grant and Lee tried to out-think each other and make strategies based on what each thought the other would do.

The Battle of the Wilderness saw some of the war's goriest fighting. Units got lost in the heavily thicketed Wilderness. Sometimes they got confused and accidentally fired on their own men. The ground was thick with dead and wounded soldiers.

The Wilderness Campaign was a draw. The Union army lost more men, about 17,000 soldiers killed or wounded. The Confederates lost about half as many men. However, Lee's casualties were more significant because he had no reinforcements. Union General Grant, on the other hand, could call on a steady stream of new recruits.

Battle of the Wilderness
Actions May 5, 1864

0   1 km
0   1 mile

- Union forces
- Confederate forces

to Germanna Ford

Spottswood

Germanna Plank Road

Spottswood Road

Lee

Wilderness Run

Wilderness Tavern

Orange Court House Turnpike

Saunders Field

Lacy (Ellwood)

Turnpike

to Chancellorsville

Higgerson

Parker's Store Road

Grant

Hickman

Battle of the Wilderness

VA

Chewning

Widow Tapp

Brock Road

to Todd's Tavern

Unfinished Railroad

Ny River

9

THE SIEGE OF PETERSBURG

Petersburg, Virginia, was a city about 20 miles (32 km) south of Richmond, the capital of the Confederacy. It was an important city with several railroads coming in and out of it. General Grant knew if he could take Petersburg, supply lines to Richmond would be cut off. Petersburg would also be a good base for Grant's planned attack on the capital.

On June 15, 1864, Grant attacked Petersburg, but his forces were stopped by Lee's army. Lee, a former engineer, decided to dig trenches for his men. This gave them needed cover, protecting them like a stone wall from Union gunfire.

The Confederate army built miles of trenches. The Union army did the same. This created a stalemate in which neither army could move against the other.

While historians call this a *siege*, it wasn't a typical siege in which a city is surrounded and the aggressors wait until the enemy runs out of food and ammunition. Petersburg was able to get supplies in and out of the city, but the armies were faced off in trenches for months. This was the first time trench warfare had been used to such a great extent. Sixty years later, trenches would be used extensively in World War I.

Soldiers dig trenches near Petersburg, Virginia.

Siege of Petersburg
Actions June 15–18, 1864

N

0   2 km
0   2 miles

■ Union forces
■ Confederate forces

Richmond Tpk

Pocahontas

Petersburg & City Point RR

Jordan Point Rd

PETERSBURG

Appomattox River

Southside RR

Harrison Creek

Siege of Petersburg

VA

Lee

Grant

Blackwater Creek

Unmanned fortifications

Norfolk & Petersburg RR

Jerusalem Plank Rd

Weldon & Petersburg RR

THE ATLANTA CAMPAIGN

Atlanta, Georgia, was the ammunitions center for the Confederacy. The city was also an important railroad hub. Union General Grant sent General William Sherman with 100,000 men to attack Atlanta.

Marching out of Chattanooga, Tennessee, Sherman moved southeast toward Atlanta. The Confederate army, under the command of General Joseph Johnston, tried to stop Sherman several times, but Sherman's superior numbers continually forced Johnston's troops to retreat.

General Joseph Johnston

Sherman marched along the railroad, since his huge army needed 14,000 tons (12,701 metric tons) of food and supplies every day to keep going.

The railroad went south and then made a turn to the west. Confederate General Johnston believed Sherman would continue following the railroad, but Sherman went farther south with as many supplies as his troops could carry. He came up behind the Confederate army, but because of quick thinking by Johnston, the Southerners managed to escape, and continued moving backwards toward Atlanta.

General William Tecumseh Sherman

Confederate President Jefferson Davis was tired of his army's constant retreat. He wanted a more aggressive general to lead the Atlanta army. General John Hood took over. He was more aggressive, but often to the point of being reckless and foolhardy. His suicidal attacks on the Union army left thousands of Confederate soldiers dead.

Union General Sherman began quietly moving his army to the other side of Atlanta. Confederate General Hood convinced himself that Sherman had left Atlanta and gone back north. Then Sherman's army attacked.

It was too late for General Hood to mount a counterattack. On September 2, 1864, Confederate General Hood deliberately detonated his own massive ammunition supplies in Atlanta, in order to keep them out of the Union's hands. At that point, Union General Sherman sent a message to Abraham Lincoln saying, "Atlanta is ours."

Afterwards, Sherman ordered the civilians of Atlanta to evacuate, and then he burned the city. Sherman was a ruthless strategist who believed that war is terribly cruel. He also believed that the crueler war was, the quicker it would be over.

The Union army captures Atlanta, but not before Confederate General Hood blows up his own massive ammunition supplies.

November 1864

SHERMAN'S MARCH TO THE SEA

After resting his weary troops in Atlanta, Union General Sherman had another task. He would march his army from Atlanta to the Atlantic Ocean, essentially cutting the Confederacy in two. He would have no way to resupply his massive army as they marched, so he decided that they could live off the land. They would eat the crops in the field, take what they needed from towns and villages, and then burn everything behind them. Sherman's ruthless plan was to cut a path 60 miles (97 km) wide through Georgia—from Atlanta to Savannah—leaving behind ruins and desolation. Sherman would destroy the South's ability to fight the war.

As the Union army marched deep through Confederate territory, they were joined by tens of thousands of freed slaves. As far as the slaves were concerned, the sight of the Union army meant freedom.

The map shows Sherman's March to the Sea, with Union forces (dark arrows) moving from Atlanta toward Savannah across Georgia, with key locations and dates:

- Atlanta, Nov 15
- Griswoldville, Nov 22
- Milledgeville, Nov 23
- Sandersville / Ball's Ferry, Nov 24-26
- Grahamville, Nov 30
- Ft. McAllister, Dec 13
- Savannah, Dec 20

Sherman's March to the Sea

Sherman's March to the Sea

N

0 — 50 km
0 — 50 miles

◼ Union forces

Sherman

The small Confederate army gave Sherman very little resistance. By the end of December 1864, the Union army reached Savannah, Georgia. After a brief fight, the Confederate army abandoned the city. Sherman had marched his Union army 300 miles (483 km) deep into Confederate territory. Now he could take his army and move north, to meet up with General Grant in Virginia.

17

THE FALLING CONFEDERACY

When Confederate General Hood lost Atlanta, Georgia, to the Union army, he moved north to lure Union General Sherman out of Georgia. Sherman did not take the bait, and continued his march toward Savannah, Georgia. General Hood, a reckless strategist, created a desperate plan to attack and retake Tennessee. In December 1864, Hood attacked the Union army at Nashville, Tennessee. The Confederate forces were soundly defeated, with more than 6,000 men killed, wounded, or captured.

Meanwhile, Sherman was marching north through South Carolina and North Carolina, destroying everything in his path. Factories, bridges, railroads, and sometimes whole villages were left in ruins. Sherman's army took horses, wagons, and anything they needed from wherever they found it. The infrastructure of the South was falling apart.

The Union blockade of Southern ports and the loss of the railroads and bridges meant that Confederate soldiers could not receive needed supplies. There were severe shortages of food and supplies all across the South. Soldiers were starving, and there was mass desertion from the Confederate ranks.

An Atlanta train depot before (above) and after (below) General Sherman's Union army destroyed it.

19

Former General George McClellan and former Congressman George Pendleton ran for president/vice president on a Democratic anti-war platform in 1864. They were soundly defeated by incumbent Republican President Abraham Lincoln and his running mate, Andrew Johnson, who wanted the Union preserved.

Abraham Lincoln was re-elected president in 1864. His opponent was former General George McClellan, the ineffective general who had been fired by Lincoln earlier in the war.

McClellan's presidential campaign was based on a Democratic Party platform. It supported ending the war immediately by recognizing the Confederacy as a separate and independent country. Lincoln won the 1864 election in a landslide, which was another blow to the Confederacy.

In February 1865, Confederate President Jefferson Davis offered a peace deal to the Union. Davis said he would send delegates to the North to construct a peace deal, but first, Abraham Lincoln had to recognize that the Confederacy was a separate and independent nation. Lincoln refused, and so the peace conference never took place.

The Confederacy was falling, and it was only a matter of time before the Union won the war. But several battles were still to be fought, including the struggle for the Confederate capital of Richmond, Virginia.

After winning a second term in office, President Lincoln (by the white podium) gave his inaugural address on March 4, 1865. He spoke of peace, but emphasized that reuniting the nation was vital.

21

April 1865

THE FALL OF RICHMOND

By the spring of 1865, Confederate General Robert E. Lee's army was dug into trenches around Petersburg, Virginia, and Richmond, Virginia, the capital of the Confederacy. Union General Grant's army was dug in also. Grant had twice as many soldiers as the Confederates, and so he dug his trenches farther and farther outward to get around the Confederate line. This meant that the Confederates had to make their front line longer, therefore thinning out the number of soldiers along the line. As the Confederate line got longer, it got weaker. One successful thrust by the Union army could break the Confederate line, and Petersburg and Richmond would fall.

Union General Sherman was coming up from the south. General Lee knew his army would soon be trapped. Lee tried to take Fort Stedman to the east of Petersburg, but suffered huge losses at the hands of Union troops.

Lee's last hope was the unit commanded by General Pickett to the southwest of Petersburg. Pickett was busy eating supper while the Union army attacked his unit. Picket did not believe that his men were being attacked until Union army officers showed up in his camp.

Union General Grant ordered a massive attack of Lee's line on April 2, 1865. The line broke, and Lee was forced to retreat. Lee informed Jefferson Davis that his army could no longer protect the capital of Richmond. Davis and his cabinet quickly fled the city.

In April 1865, Union troops were about to enter Richmond. Many people fled the Confederacy's capital city, including President Jefferson Davis and his cabinet. The Confederate army was ordered to destroy anything that might benefit the Union army. Tobacco, cotton, clothing, and food supplies were set on fire. Starving citizens tried desperately to take some of the supplies. Flames spread and grew out of control. Parts of Richmond burned because of fires set by their own army.

April 9, 1865

SURRENDER AT APPOMATTOX

After retreating from Richmond and Petersburg, Virginia, General Lee's army moved west. His men were starving, exhausted, and waiting for supplies and food that never came. Union General Grant sent Lee a message. He said that he wanted to spill no more blood, and asked Lee to surrender.

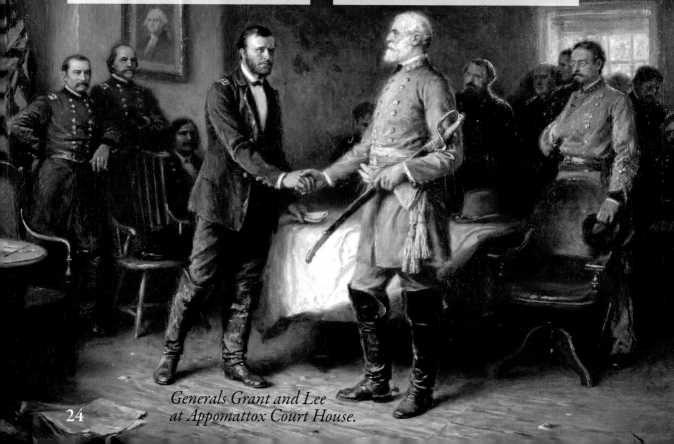

Generals Grant and Lee at Appomattox Court House.

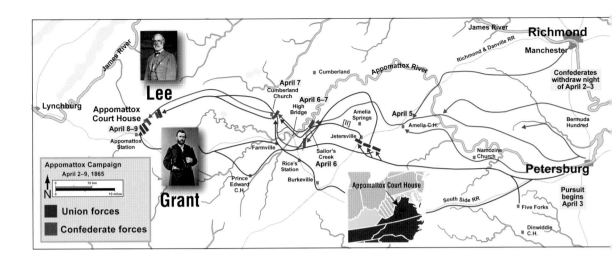

General Lee reached the village of Appomattox Court House, Virginia, hoping to escape with his army of 18,000 men. But he found that his small, weakened army was surrounded by a massive, well-equipped, well-fed Union army. Lee was forced to surrender.

On April 9, 1865, in the front parlor of the McLean House in Appomattox Court House, General Grant and General Lee met. Grant said that if the Confederate soldiers would lay down their weapons, they would be allowed to go home. Lee asked that his men be able to keep their horses,

as they would be necessary for spring planting. Grant agreed. Grant ordered that the Confederate soldiers be fed, and also ordered his own men not to celebrate the end of the war. "The rebels are our countrymen again," Grant said. As the Confederate soldiers marched in line to give up their weapons, the Union troops were ordered to stand at attention and give a salute to their countrymen.

The formal day of surrender was April 12, 1865. It was four years—to the day—of the first shots of the war at Fort Sumter, South Carolina.

April 14, 1865

Booth's Deringer

LINCOLN ASSASSINATED

With the fighting over, President Abraham Lincoln was busy planning how to create one unified country again. He wanted to help the Southern states rebuild, and welcome them back without animosity, punishment, or revenge. However, after the horror of 625,000 Americans dead in the Civil War, there would be one more national tragedy.

Two days after the official surrender of the Confederate army, Abraham Lincoln and his wife were attending a play at Ford's Theatre in Washington, D.C. John Wilkes Booth, a white supremacist and Confederate supporter, snuck up behind Lincoln and shot him in the head. Abraham Lincoln received a fatal wound, and died the next morning.

John Wilkes Booth escaped the city, but he was caught and killed by Union troops 12 days later at a farm in rural Virginia. John Wilkes Booth was part of a small group who thought they could throw the American government into chaos by assassinating Lincoln and several of his cabinet members. Their plan failed. Eight of Booth's coconspirators were captured, tried and convicted, and four were hanged.

President Lincoln was shot at Ford's Theatre by John Wilkes Booth on the night of April 14, 1865. Unconscious, Lincoln was carried across the street to a nearby home. The president died there at 7:22 am the next morning.

RECONSTRUCTION

After Abraham Lincoln's assassination, Vice President Andrew Johnson became president. Lincoln's plans for unifying the country were tossed out. President Johnson was a hard-line Unionist who was less interested in peaceful unification. Abraham Lincoln is regarded by historians as one of the best—if not *the* best—presidents in history. Andrew Johnson is often regarded as one of the worst.

President Andrew Johnson

The post-Civil War years should have been a new era for the United States. Instead, poor political leadership and continued prejudice against African Americans hindered the attempts made to reunify and rebuild the country.

Andrew Johnson spent most of his presidency in petty bickering with Congress. Congress attempted to remove him from office, but without success. Without the great personal leadership of Abraham Lincoln, the country accomplished very little to help the Southern states rebuild their economy and infrastructure.

Although the slaves were now officially free, they still faced huge obstacles in the years following the Civil War. Prejudice and discrimination were common. Many former slaves, although free, had nowhere to go, and the Southern economy was in ruins. African Americans would have to wait for decades until the government passed laws to give them their full civil rights.

Freed slaves faced ongoing prejudice. Many found themselves without jobs and with nowhere to go.

GLOSSARY

ABOLITIONISTS

Those who were anti-slavery, and believed that slavery was morally wrong.

CAMPAIGN

An organized way to achieve a specific goal. A campaign may refer to a military action, such as the Wilderness Campaign. It may also refer to a political candidate's attempt to win an elected office, such as the office of the president of the United States.

CIVIL WAR

A war where two parts of the same nation fight against each other. The American Civil War was fought between Northern and Southern states from 1861–1865. The Southern states were for slavery. They wanted to start their own country. Northern states fought against slavery and a division of the country.

CONFEDERACY

The Southern states of Alabama, Arkansas, Florida, Georgia, Louisiana, Mississippi, North Carolina, South Carolina, Tennessee, Texas, and Virginia. These states wanted to keep slavery legal. They broke away from the United States during the Civil War and formed their own country known as the Confederate States of America, or simply the Confederacy. The Confederacy ended in 1865 when the war ended and the 11 Confederate states rejoined the United States.

EMANCIPATION PROCLAMATION
President Abraham Lincoln's September 1862 declaration that freed slaves in states still in rebellion against the United States.

RECONSTRUCTION
A period of time after the Civil War during which the ruined Southern states were rebuilt. Reconstruction was made more difficult because of President Lincoln's assassination a few days after the end of the war.

SIEGE
Surrounding a city or fortification, and then waiting for people inside to run out of food and supplies.

UNION
The Northern states united against the Confederacy. "Union" also refers to all of the states of the United States. President Lincoln wanted to preserve the Union, keeping the Northern and Southern states together.

WHITE SUPREMACIST
A person who believes that white-skinned people are superior to people of other skin colors, particularly people of African descent.

WORLD WAR I
A war that was fought in Europe from 1914 to 1918, involving countries around the world. Great Britain, France, Russia, and Italy (the Allies) opposed the Central Powers (Germany, Austria-Hungary, Turkey, and Bulgaria). The United States entered the war in April 1917 on the side of the Allies.

INDEX